OFF the BONE

OFF the BONE

by GRIFF.

WARNER BOOKS

A *Warner* Book

First published in Great Britain in 1996

A CIP catalogue record for this book
is available from the British Library.

ISBN 0 7515 1458 6

Printed in England by Clays Ltd, St Ives plc

Warner Books
A Division of
Little, Brown and Company (UK)
Brettenham House
Lancaster Place
London WC2E 7EN

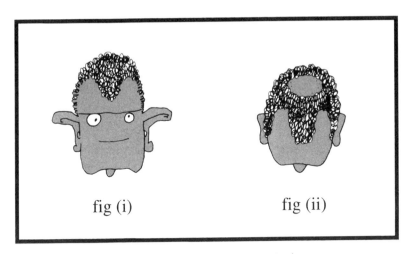

fig (i)   fig (ii)

Male Pattern Baldness

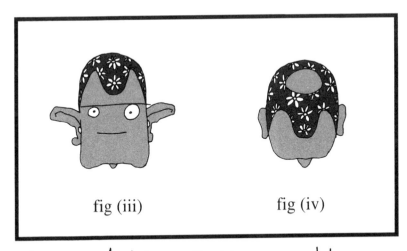

fig (iii)   fig (iv)

Laura Ashley Pattern Baldness

The first and only meeting
of the ill-fated support group,
Attention-Seekers Anonymous.

BANANA SAFETY

1. Grip tightly, with fruit curving away from the body.
2. Wait quietly until help arrives.

Bernard had chosen
a breakfast with a
degree of difficulty
of 5.85.

If metalwork was fun...

"Right Kids — today we add a Stun/Maim Toggle Switch to the electric cattle prods we started last week."

Every Monday morning,
Vera calls in at the corner-shop
to see if chocolate-flavour crisps
have been invented yet.

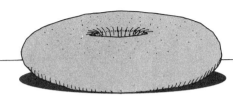

In De Niro's
most challenging role to date,
he plays a ring doughnut
in Scorsese's
"Tales From a Patisserie".

Another dinner party anecdote gets out of hand.

Don't do anything silly, Mr Harris.

a
b
c

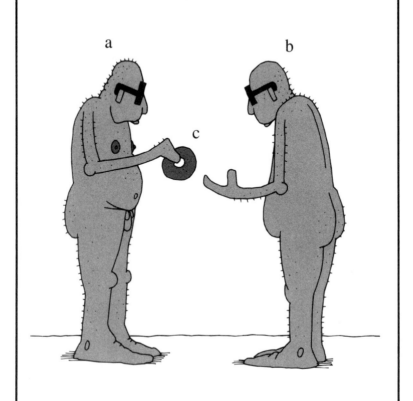

a Donor
b Donee
c Donut

Key Moments in Rock History

3/8/72

Elvis tries his first burger.

Any moment now,
a gentle squeeze of the trigger
would unload a pint-and-a-half
of Evening Primrose Oil
into Deidre's rump.

This was something
altogether new —
flies working in pairs.

Carruthers made a mental note
not to use "Giggler" Harris
on these next-of-kin
assignments in future.

It took at least 8 gruelling
   hours of sweat-soaked straining
and discomfort to bring each
of my children into this world.

And that was
   just the sex.

Norman discovers
a shampoo which gives
his hair more body.

This wasn't the first time
that Dimchurch had misjudged
his interview-wear.

This wasn't the first time
that Dimchurch had misjudged
his interview-wear.

Right Dallas book
depository,
wrong attaché case.

It was beginning
to look as if Bernard's
medication might need
tweaking again.

Your Personal Organiser as an Anti-Mugging Device

Make a drinks date
for a Week-on-Thursday,
and then fail to show.

" New term, new start...
... what do you say, kids? "

"I made it in woodwork, dad.
It started off as a CD player,
but now it removes nostril hair."

Bernard is allowed
to put one question
to God.

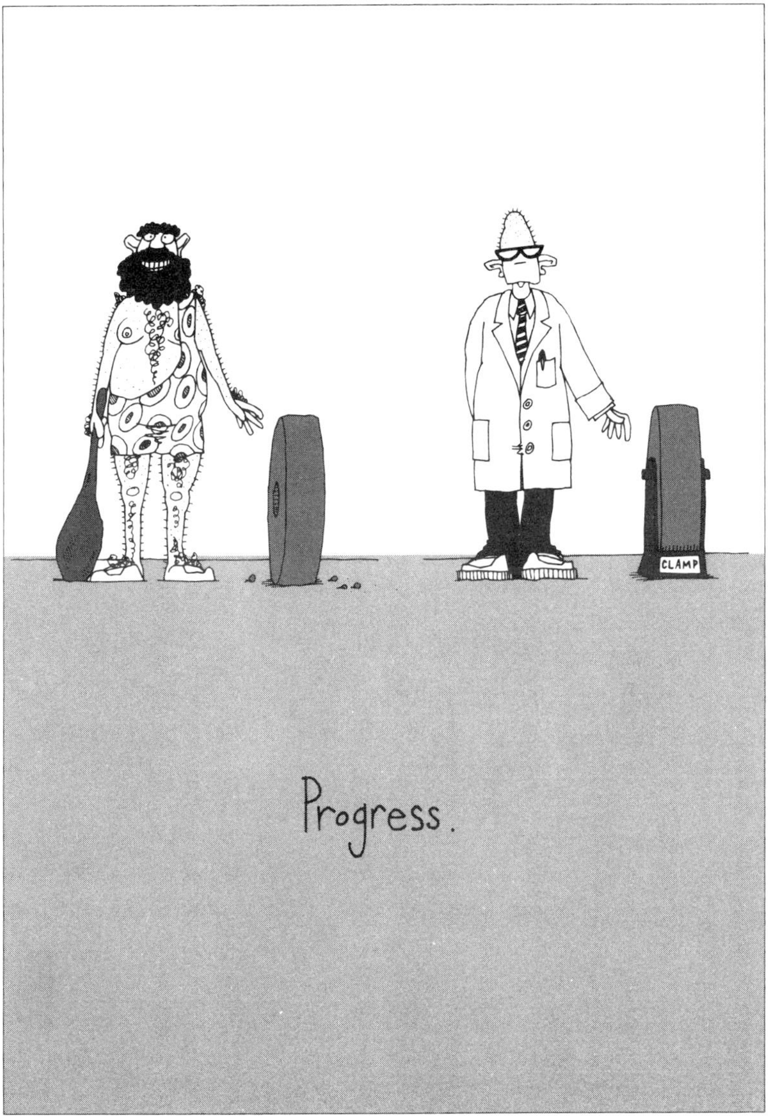
CLAMP
Progress.

It is a little known fact
that the film 'Psycho'
was originally intended
for a U-certificate.

ouch.

The first draft
of the shower scene
involved a lady
slipping on the soap
and badly
bruising her knee.

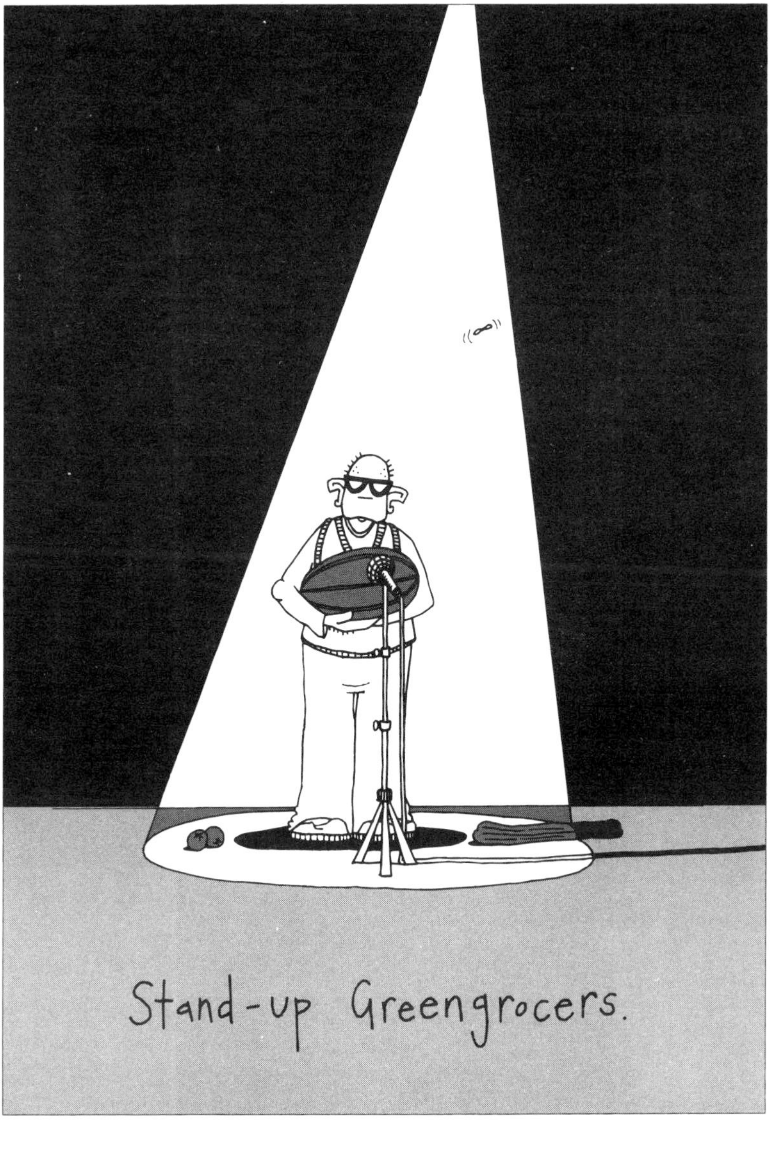
Stand-up Greengrocers.

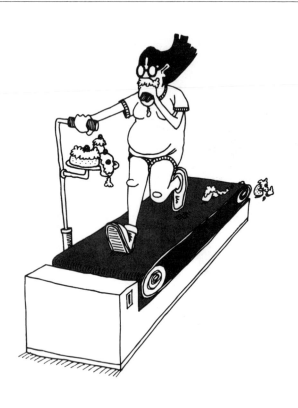

Deidre had achieved
'Steady State'.

Supply teachers.
Smell the fear.

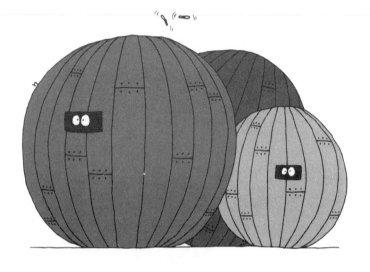

Trojan Horse poo.

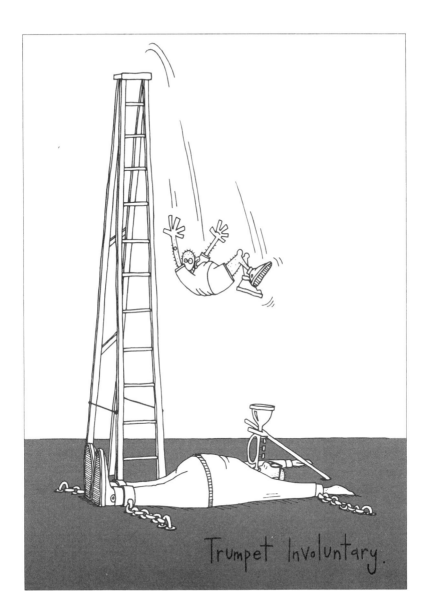

Trumpet Involuntary.

Malcolm was beginning
to dread Tuesday nights.

"Hmm...
Something to
help with your
bed-wetting problem,
you say...
...what an
unusual request..."

Playing Father Christmas was
giving Mr Purkiss a warmer
feeling than usual this year.

In an unlikely sponsorship deal,
it was agreed that gang members
would have 'LOVE' tattoo'd
on the knuckles of one hand,
and 'SPAM' on the other.

"Well, the news is mixed, Mr Harris.
Your sperm count is low,
but the ones you **do** have
are chipper little fellows."

The String Vest
Collection.

Derek attempts to patent
a water-cannon
for breaking up very minor
public disturbances.

Film Sequels Which Bombed

 No. 12 Plays Scrabble With Wolves.

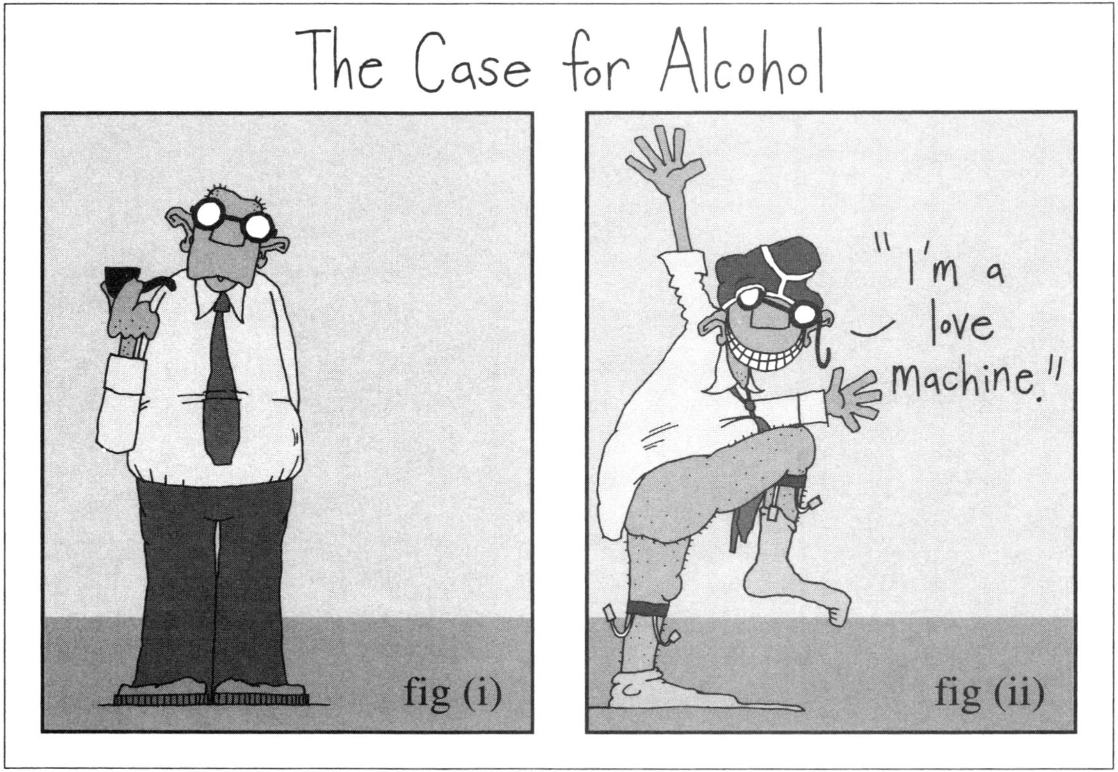
The Case for Alcohol
fig (i)
"I'm a love machine."
fig (ii)

Elsie considered her
husband's allergy a small
price to pay for the
enjoyment she got
from Snuffles.

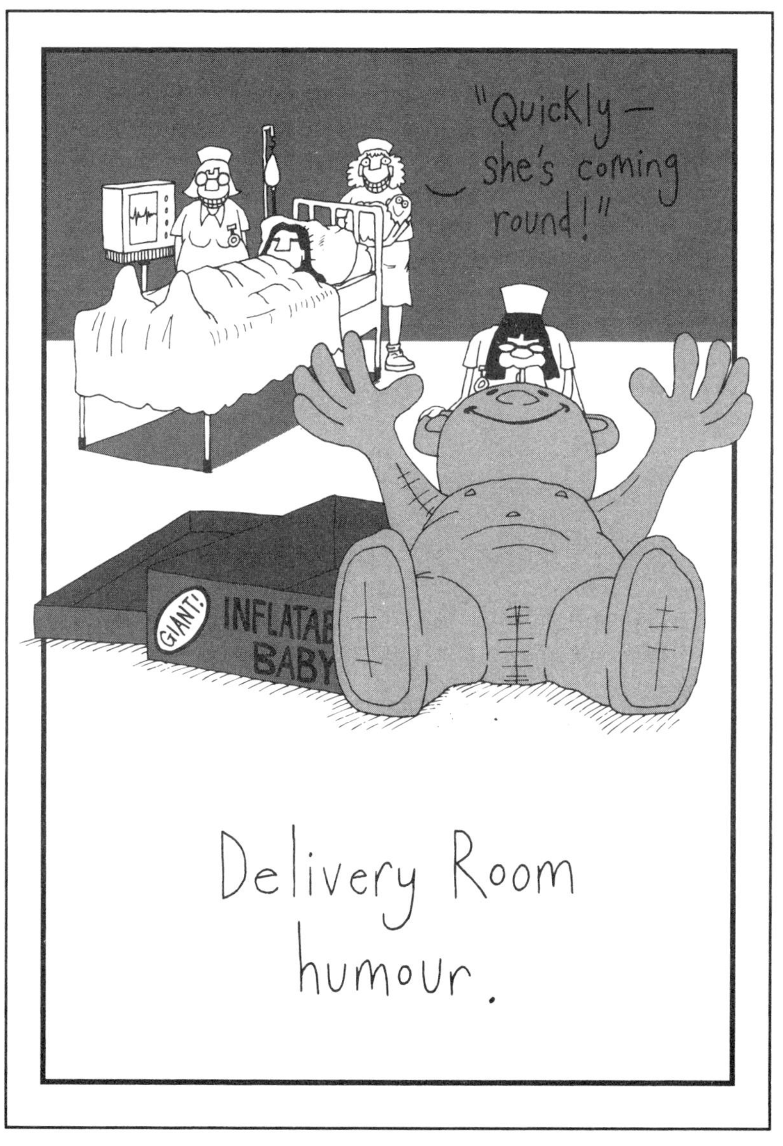
"Quickly — she's coming round!"
GIANT!
INFLATAB
BABY

Delivery Room humour.

Unfriendly
Barber.

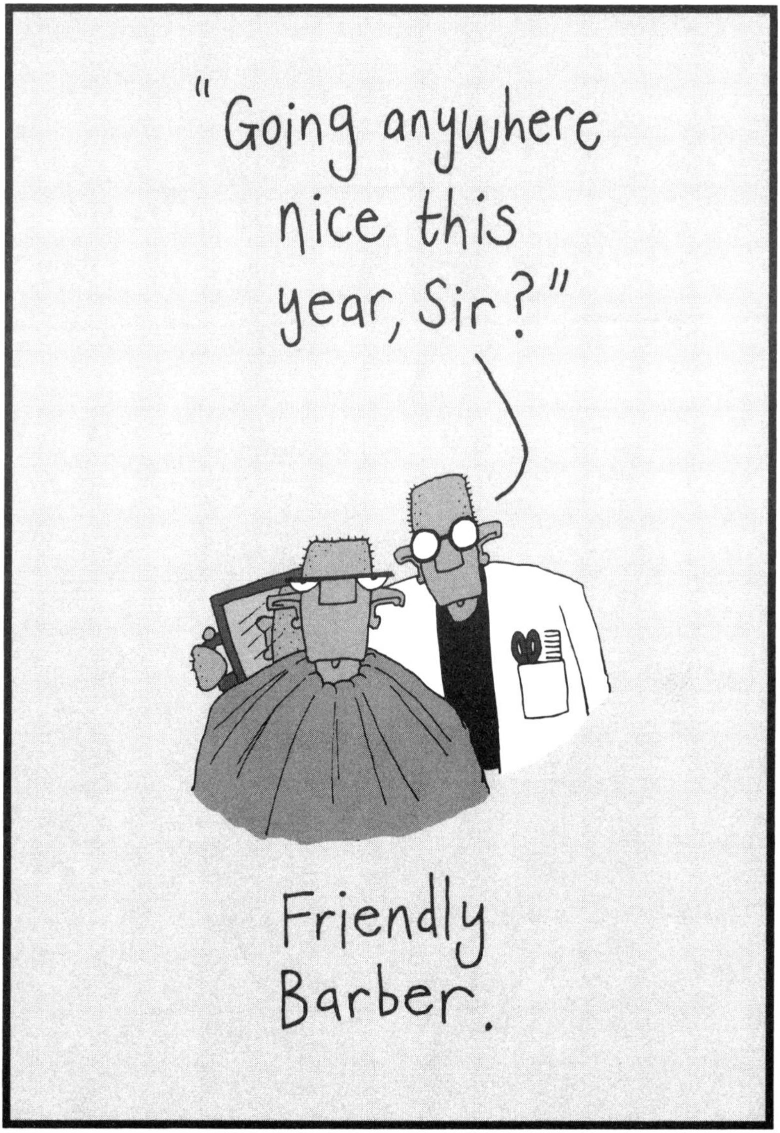
"Going anywhere nice this year, Sir?"
Friendly Barber.

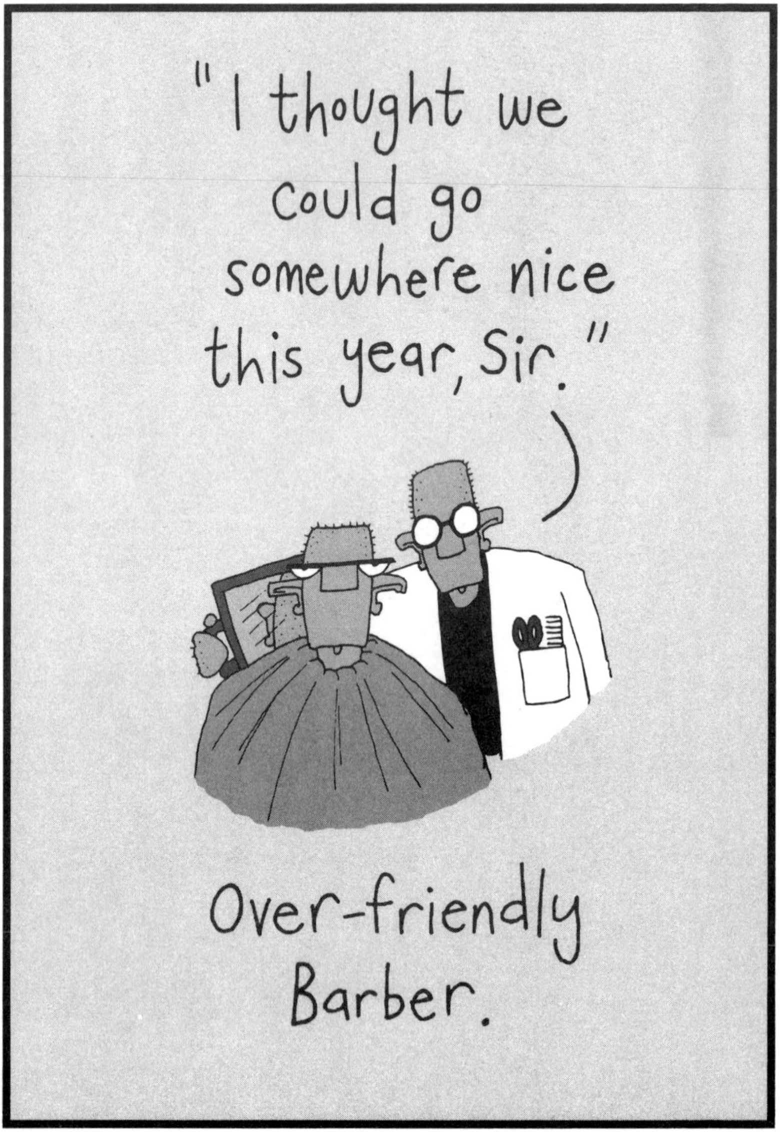
"I thought we could go somewhere nice this year, Sir."

Over-friendly Barber.

It looked like Roger
may have over-estimated
the strength of his
bargaining position on this one.

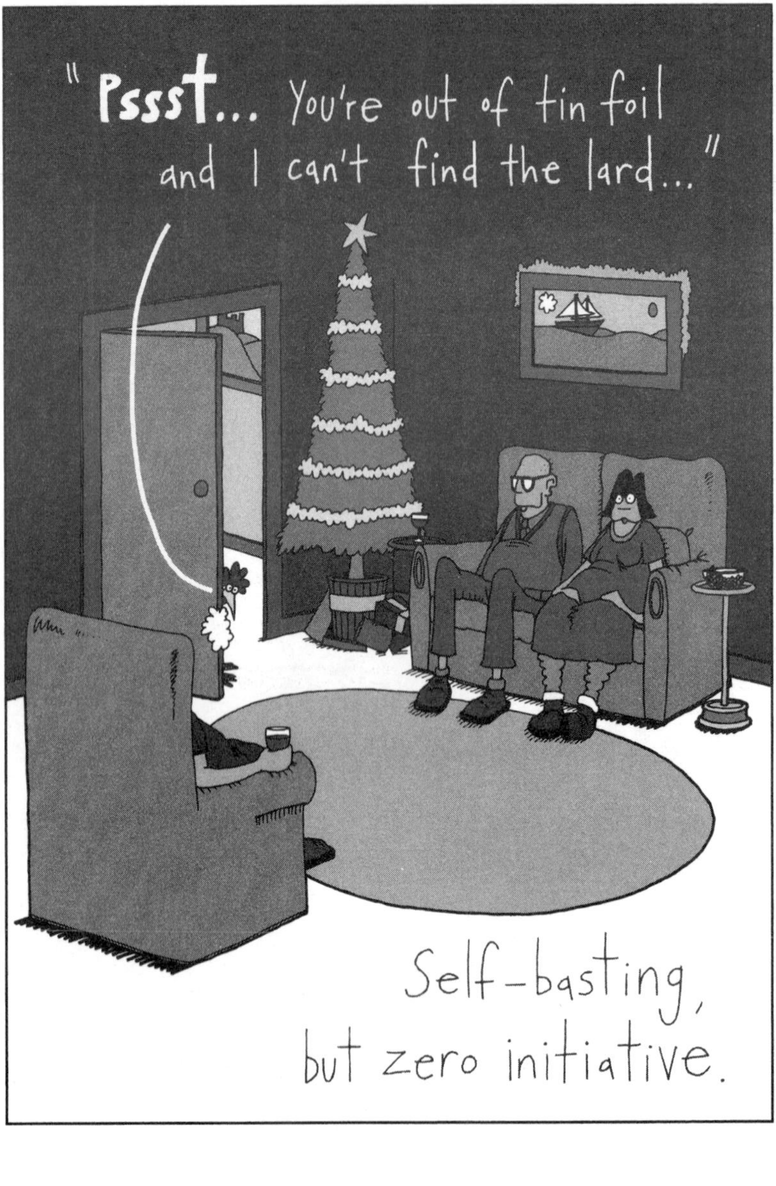
"Pssst... You're out of tin foil and I can't find the lard..."
Self-basting, but zero initiative.

There **are** men, of course,
who claim that dressing up
in women's underwear
is no fun at all.

They usually just need
to move up a bra size.

Vera was of the
"If in doubt, blend it"
school of cookery.

It looked ominous —
Vera had strapped on her
Row-Booster Pack, and
was about to engage
Logic Override.

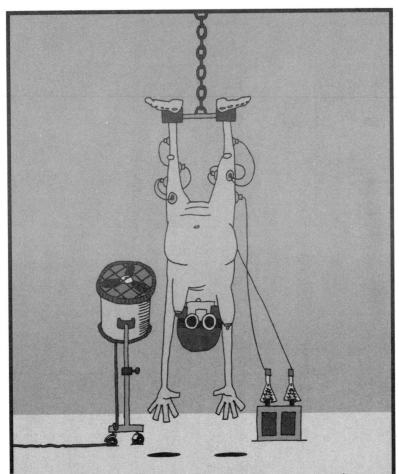

Doreen's cellulite battle
was hotting up.

"I'm sorry Jarvis,
but unless your hands improve
I'm going to have to give
the chalk to someone else.

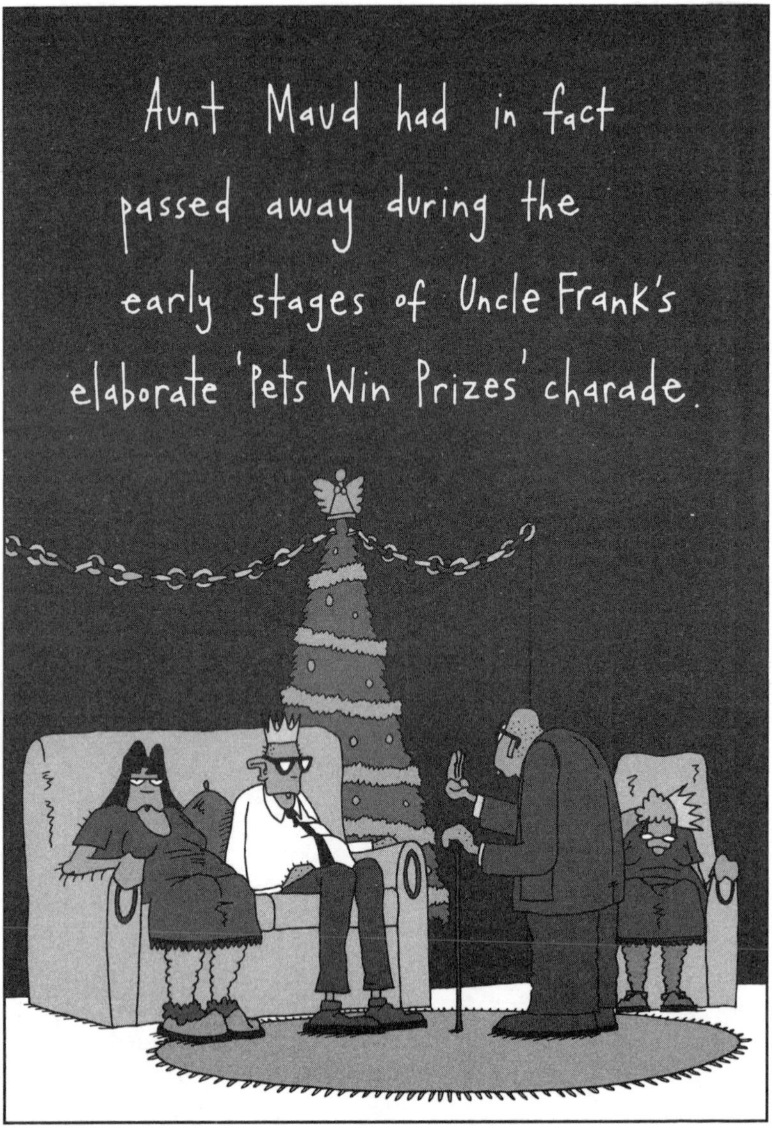
Aunt Maud had in fact passed away during the early stages of Uncle Frank's elaborate 'Pets Win Prizes' charade.

Black countered
with the rarely-seen
Reverse-Moony defence.

Mr Purkiss had found Vera's
secret chocolate store,
and now he must die.

Statistics show that up to
93% of all domestic violence
is 'chocolate related'.

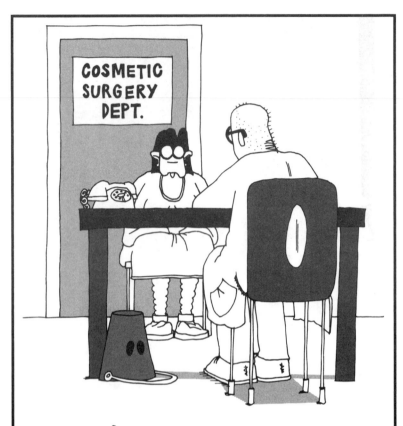

Dr Boffmeister always liked
to break the ice
with his "Budget Special" gag.

Inferior-Novelty Complex

The irrational belief
that you've
come off worst
in the cracker-pull again.

"What's black and white
and red all over?
I don't know but, boy,
have you got a fat arse."

Offensive Christmas crackers.

It was an unusual yet strangely compelling defence.

God puts his design plans
before the Board.

Dinner Party Tips

No. 54

Even prolonged conversational lulls
need not be awkward, provided
suitable arrangements have been made.

Happiness is
a chocolate drip.

The Elephant Man discovers
that his hair-line has
begun to recede.

Having eaten 12 satsumas,
1½ lb of stuffing and
the fairy off the Christmas tree,
Aunt Vera had to be
blown up by the police
in a controlled explosion.

The other Superheroes were getting tired of Flatulence Man blaming his mysterious side-kick, Captain Invisible.

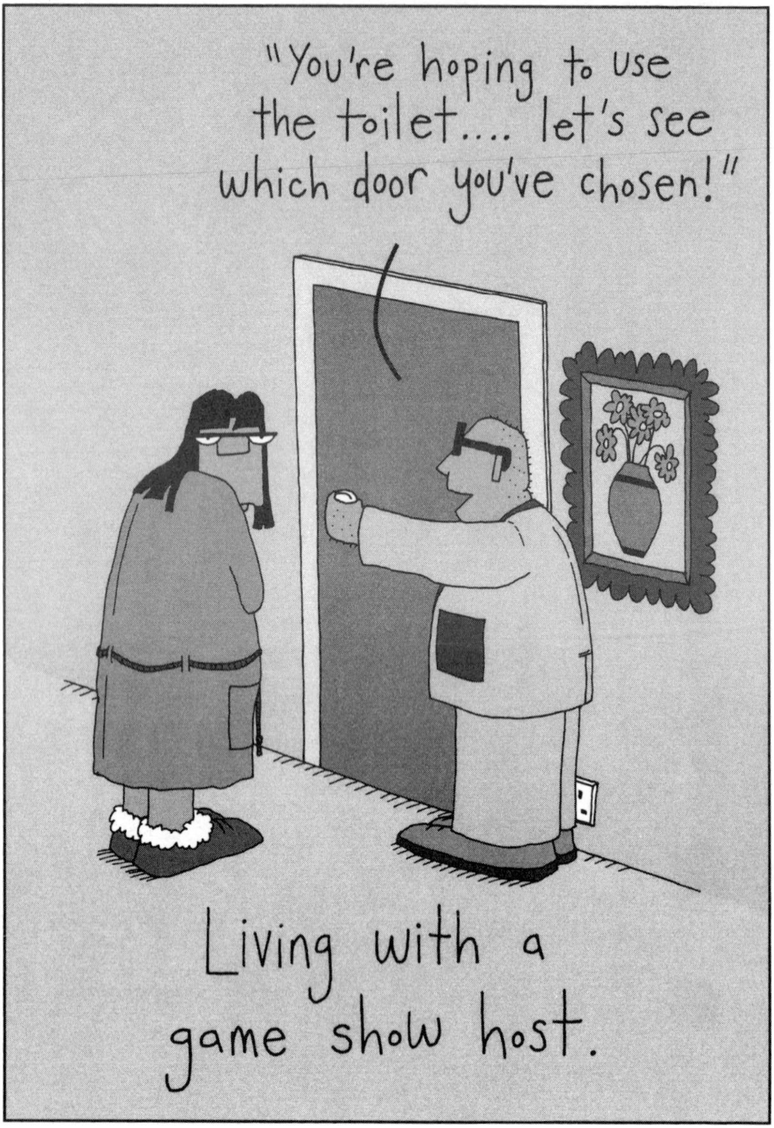
"You're hoping to use the toilet.... let's see which door you've chosen!"
Living with a game show host.

"Norman Spokes.
Age 40.
Must try harder."
If God gave
end-of-term reports.

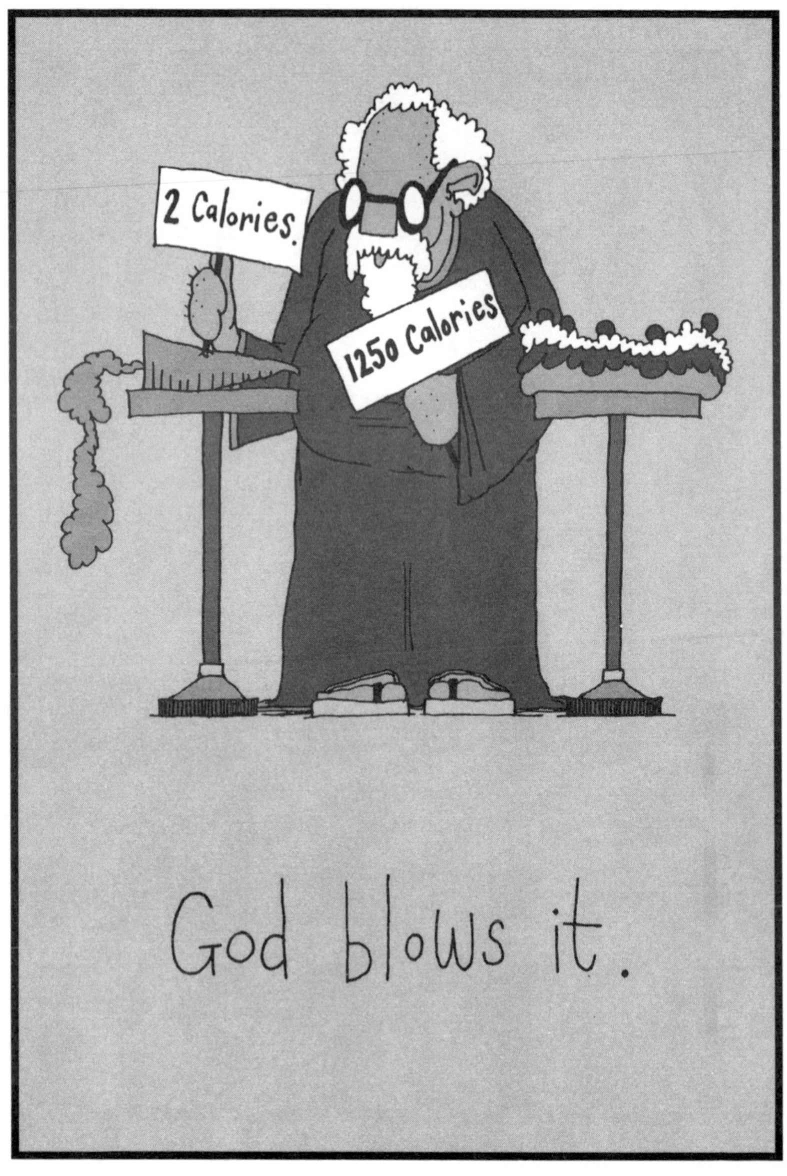
2 Calories.
1250 Calories

God blows it.

Of all the bars, in all the world, she had to walk in during Fez 'n' Frills Happy Hour.

Houdini tries to change his duvet cover.

Clive sensed that the interview was slipping away from him.

Deidre had ironed
one too many of
her husband's shirts.

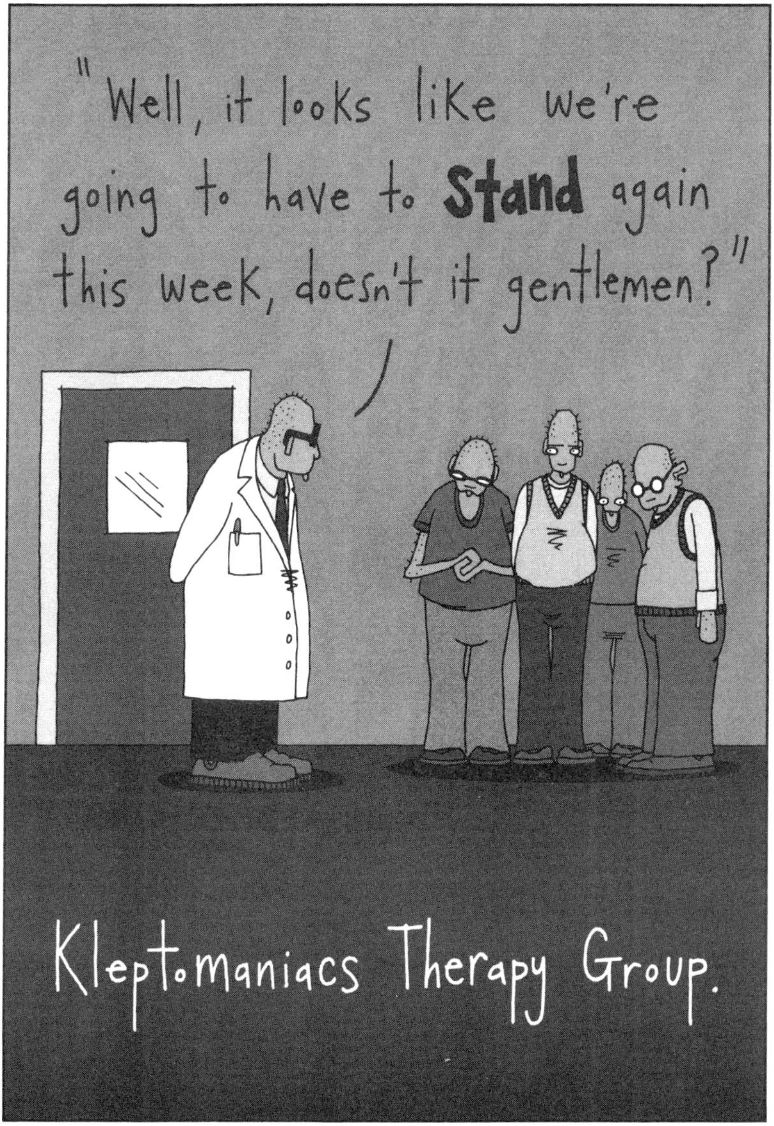
"Well, it looks like we're going to have to Stand again this week, doesn't it gentlemen?"
Kleptomaniacs Therapy Group.

It smacked of one of George's
last-minute presents —
a bottle of windscreen wash,
two cans of multi-grade
and 15 packs of chewing gum.

Ralph had been caught
trying to bury the last
of the turkey left-overs.

Liposuction Basics

Check and **double-check** that Suck/Blow switch.

The Male Menopause
Spotting the Warning Signs

fig (i)

fig (ii)

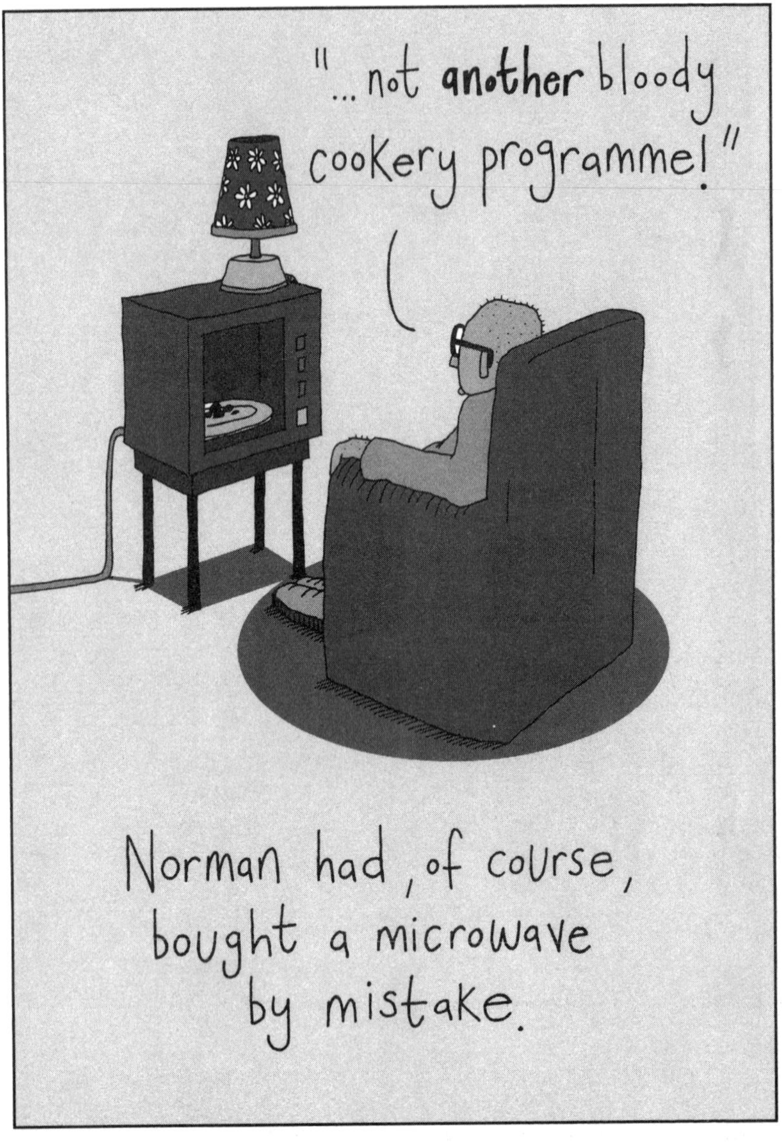
"... not **another** bloody cookery programme!"

Norman had, of course, bought a microwave by mistake.

"Well, the good news is we've persuaded Mr Glenn Miller to play us a little something....

....the bad news is there looks like some turbulence ahead..."

It was to become known
as the year of
the Great Gift-Tag Mix-up.

By the age
of 14
Mozart had
written
25 concertos
and 6 operas.

Duncan, on the other hand,
can reach level 46 of
Manic Astro-Gherkins Trash Venus.

"Now tell me there's no room at the inn, sucker."
"Cool! Eat your myrhh and you get 8 bonus wise men."
bam
bop
NATIVITY CARNAGE III

There are those, of course,
who feel an award for
speed-eating doughnuts lowers
the tone of the whole event.

It soon became clear that Mr Purkiss was playing a percentage game.

It was the oldest interrogation
technique in the book —
one officer acting tough, the other
wearing tight leather shorts and
flirting outrageously.

In a horrific seasoning accident, Luigi is crushed under his own novelty pepper grinder.

"I'll be with you in a moment, Mrs Harris..."

Dr Boffhausen was breaking new ground with his work on phobias.

Carruthers had been
caught photocopying
root vegetables again.

"I have Keenly been studying your fleshy buttocks, madam."
Sven's phrase book was getting him into hot water again.

"Good afternoon ladies and gentlemen, this is your baggage-handler speaking...."

The airline's new "responsibility-sharing" policy was spooking some of the passengers.

A quick glance at his
Pre-Menstrual Timepiece
confirmed Vern's worst fears.

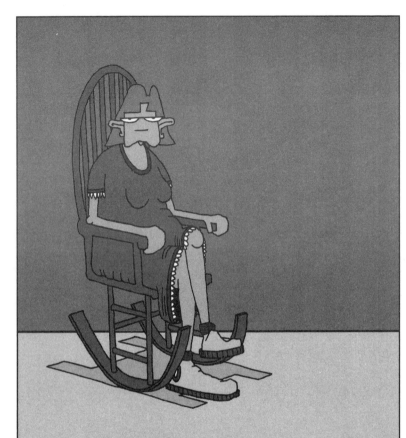

Well that's puberty over.
Let the ageing process begin.

Quasimodo tries
to de-emphasise
using stripes.

"Would you still love me
if I had a pillow growing
out of my head?"

Malcolm still needed
constant reassurance.

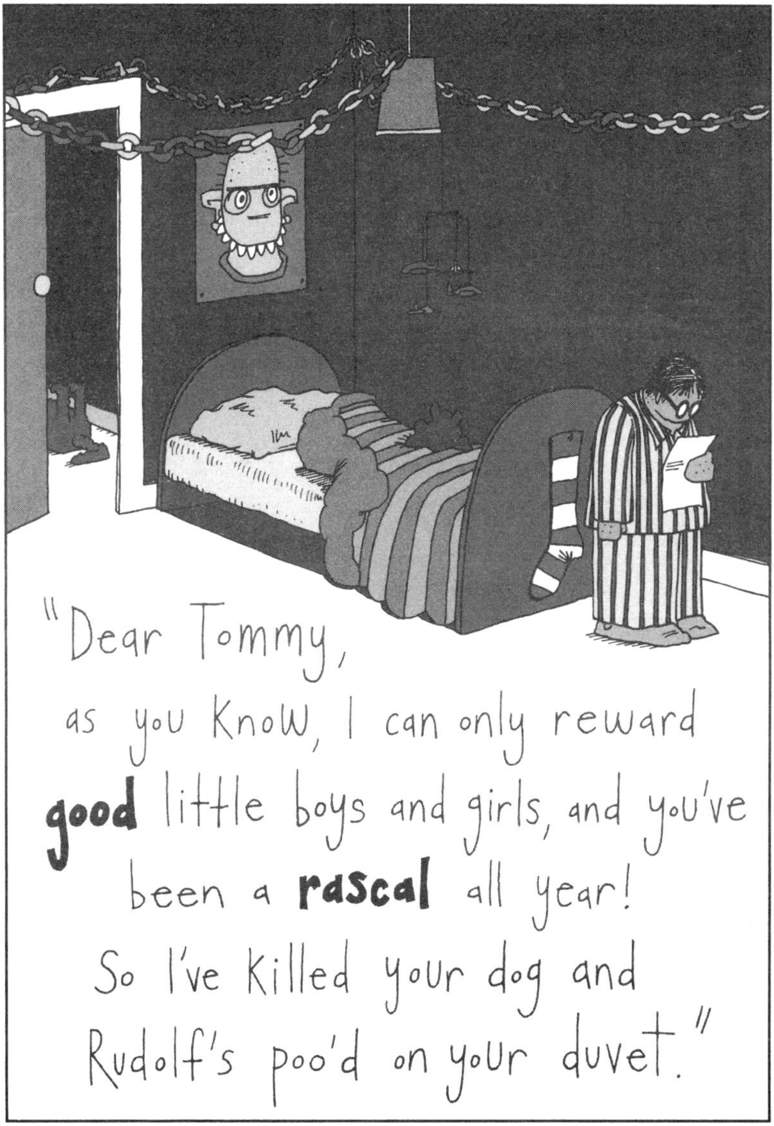
"Dear Tommy,
as you know, I can only reward
good little boys and girls, and you've
been a rascal all year!
So I've killed your dog and
Rudolf's poo'd on your duvet."

Over the years,
Vera had found how to
get the best from
her bathroom scales.

Stranded in the
jungle as an infant,
Mr Purkiss had been
raised by wild sloths.

Norman. Trainspotter specialising in locomotives of the 1940s and '50s.

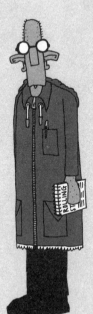

Roger. Trainspotter specialising in buffet cars.

"It's so often the simple things in life that give the most pleasure," mused Nora, as she switched on her wind machine.

Unsuccessful attempt
to break down
sexual stereotypes.

"Well this should get a few
bums back on pews," thought
Reverend Puttock, triumphantly.

This wasn't the first time that
Olive had tried to make off
with the entire dessert trolley.

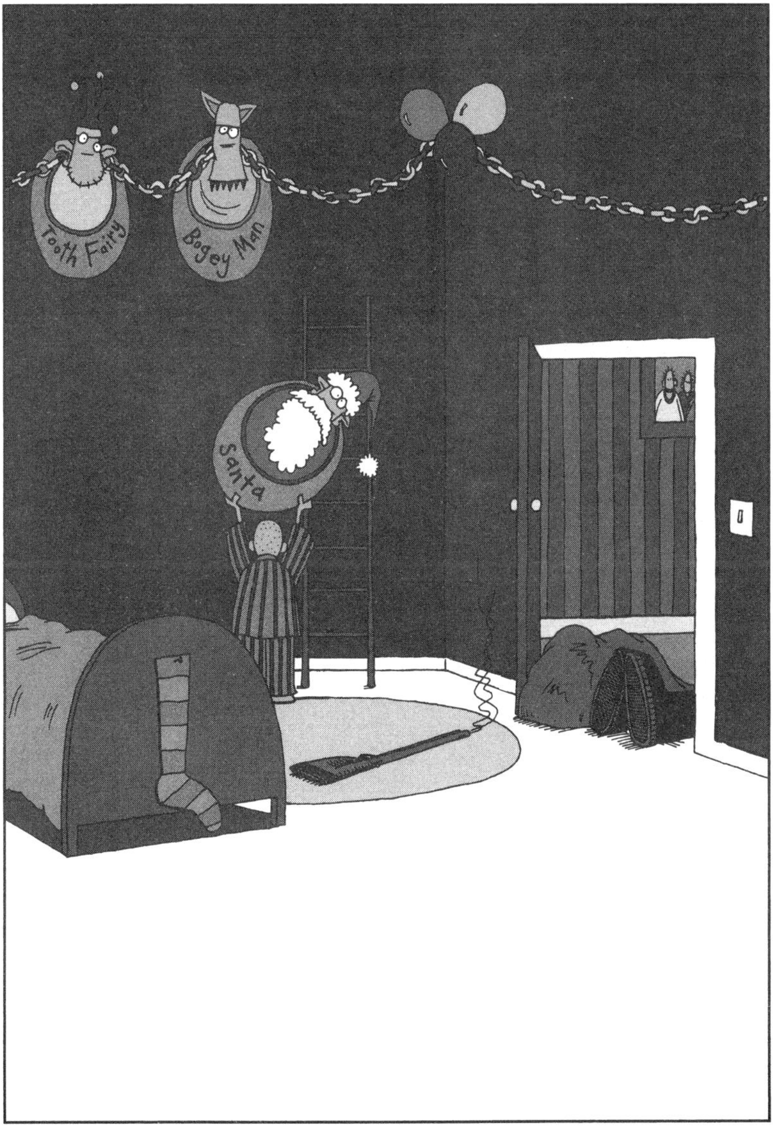
Tooth Fairy
Bogey Man
Santa

"I hope this **is** a dream," worried Nigel, "or I'm going to have a terrible job getting the whipped cream out of the carpet."

The previous night's
wife-swapping party
had gone horribly wrong.

Wayne is 2 million years
and 7 minutes too late.

Life Strategies

Speak softly and carry a 12" pizza in your hand-bag.

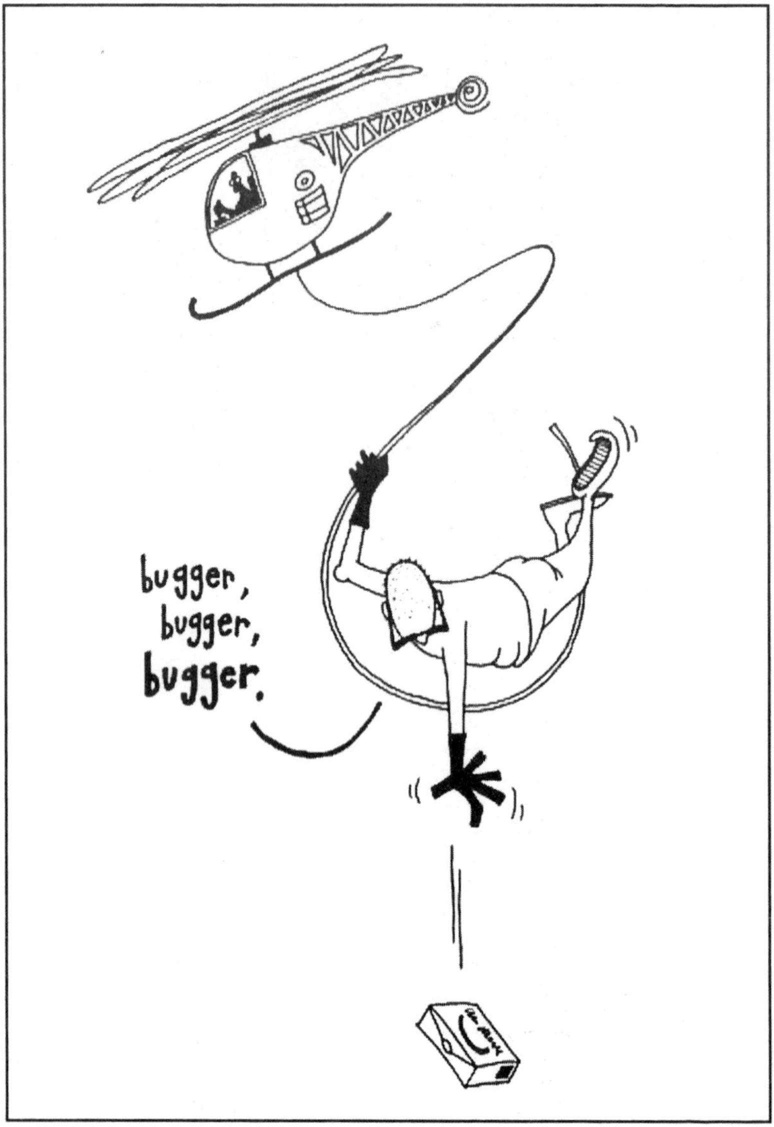
bugger,
bugger,
bugger.

Every month, Vera sends a small
donation supporting
research into the elusive
triple-chocolate chip muffin.

Gwenda tries to add a
cream cakes section
to her personal organiser.

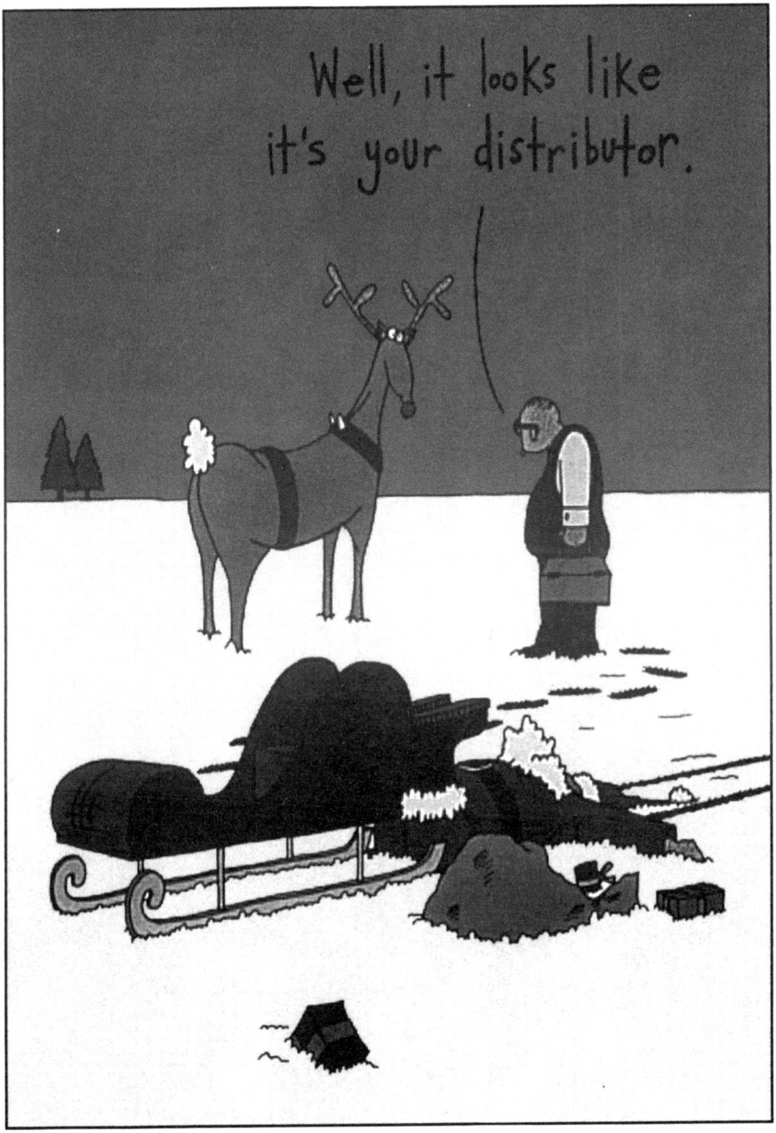
Well, it looks like
it's your distributor.

"Shortly, Sir, I shall tap my clipboard on the dash, leap out of the vehicle, and make my way back to the test centre by tube and bus."

The feeding frenzy over,
Deidre retreats to her lair.

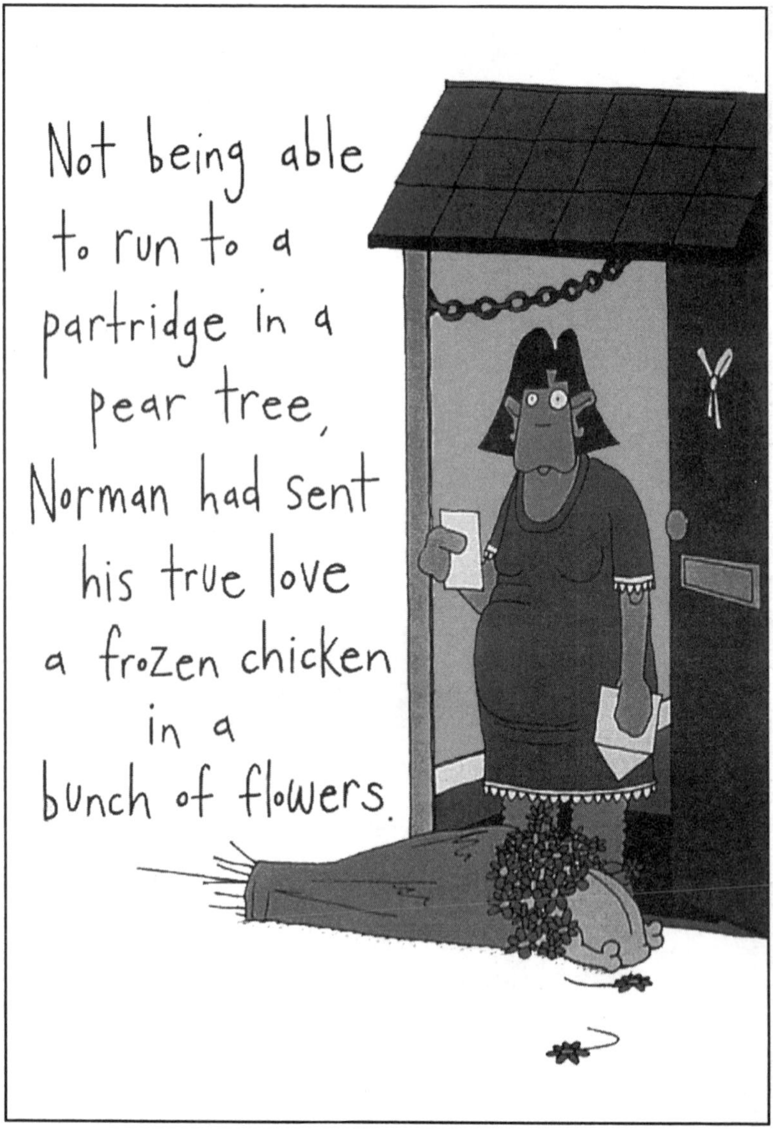
Not being able to run to a partridge in a pear tree, Norman had sent his true love a frozen chicken in a bunch of flowers.

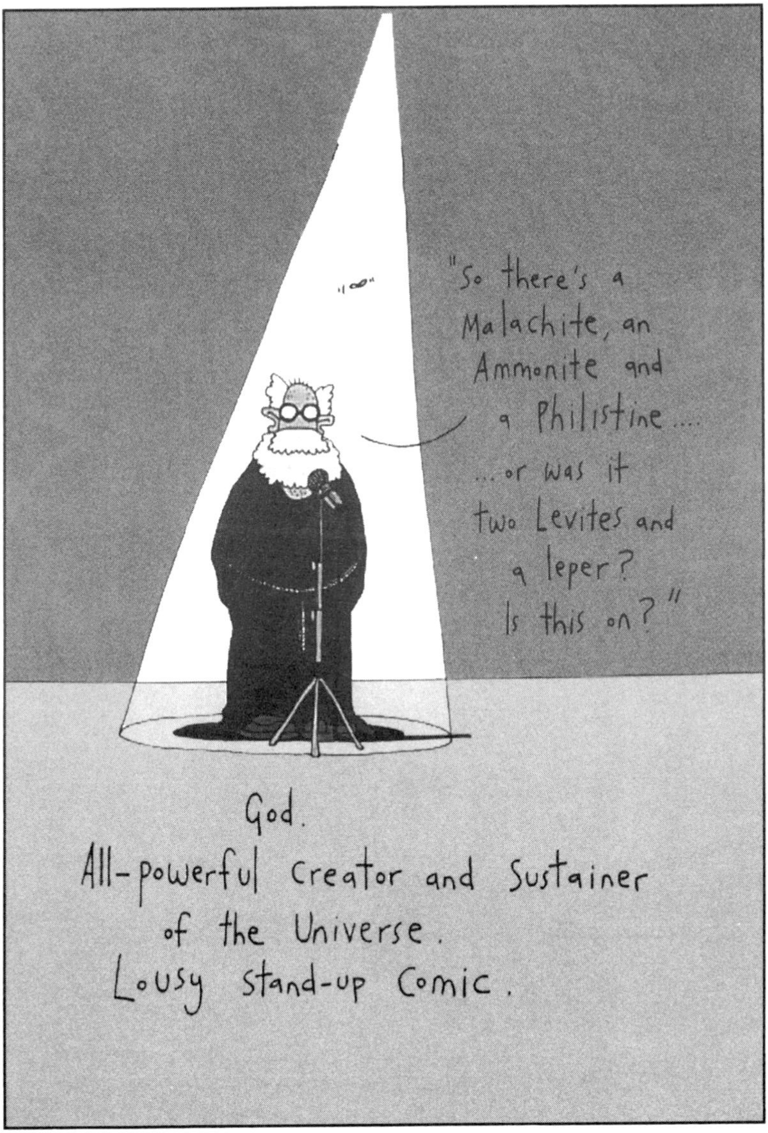
"So there's a Malachite, an Ammonite and a Philistine.... ...or was it two Levites and a leper? Is this on?"
God.
All-powerful creator and Sustainer of the Universe.
Lousy stand-up comic.

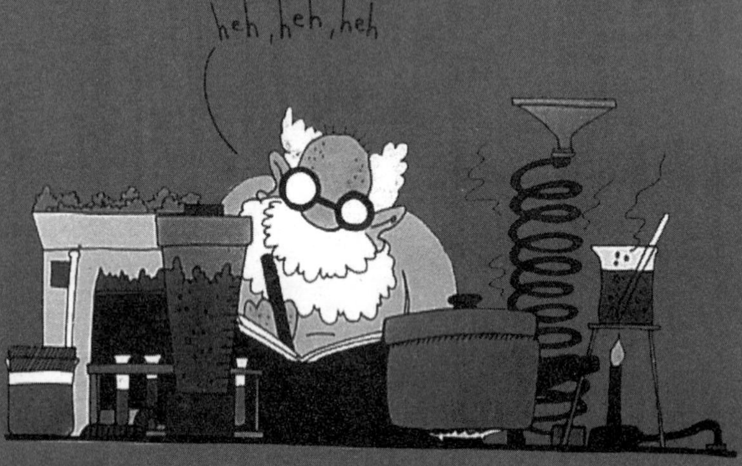
heh, heh, heh

God creates cellulite.

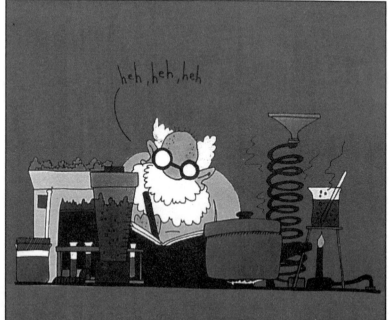

That critical moment in
a man's life when, for the first
time, he has more hair on
his bum than his head.

Every year, Mad Uncle Frank would doze off during the Queen's speech, and wake up at the end of The Great Escape.

Negotiations broke down
after 4½ hours.
Tommy was prepared to lose
the shire horse and the hovercraft,
but he still wouldn't budge on
the Stealth Bomber.

"I know 26 verses of Silent Night
and Darren's never had a
saxophone lesson in his life.
Do the sensible thing, Mrs Harris."

"The headlines once more....

...Bob the camera man's
   got prostate trouble,
   and my Y-fronts
   are pinching big-time."

It was what they call
a 'slow news day.'

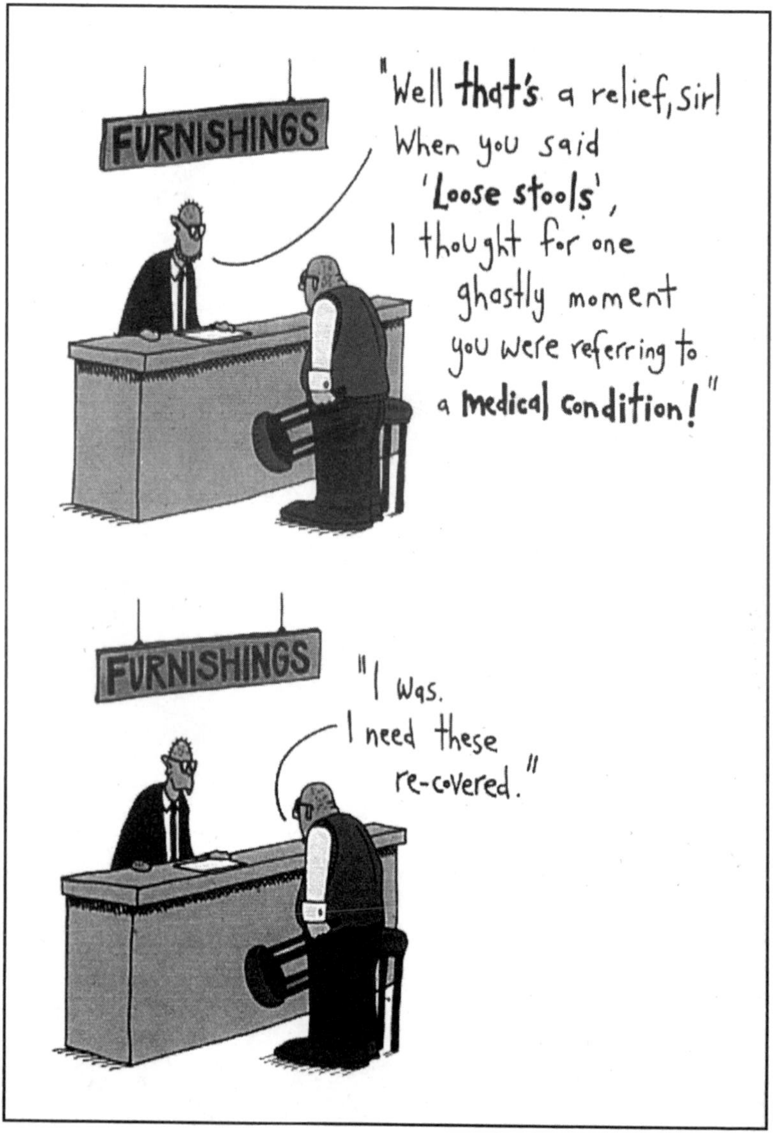
FURNISHINGS
"Well that's a relief, sir! When you said 'Loose stools', I thought for one ghastly moment you were referring to a medical condition!"
FURNISHINGS
"I was. I need these re-covered."

Little did Doreen know that
Roger had already removed
all the tangerine creams,
and was at that moment
boarding a plane to Brazil.

Slasher had baffled the rest of the Chapter with his 3-piece suite tattoo.

Two wise men.
One dummy.

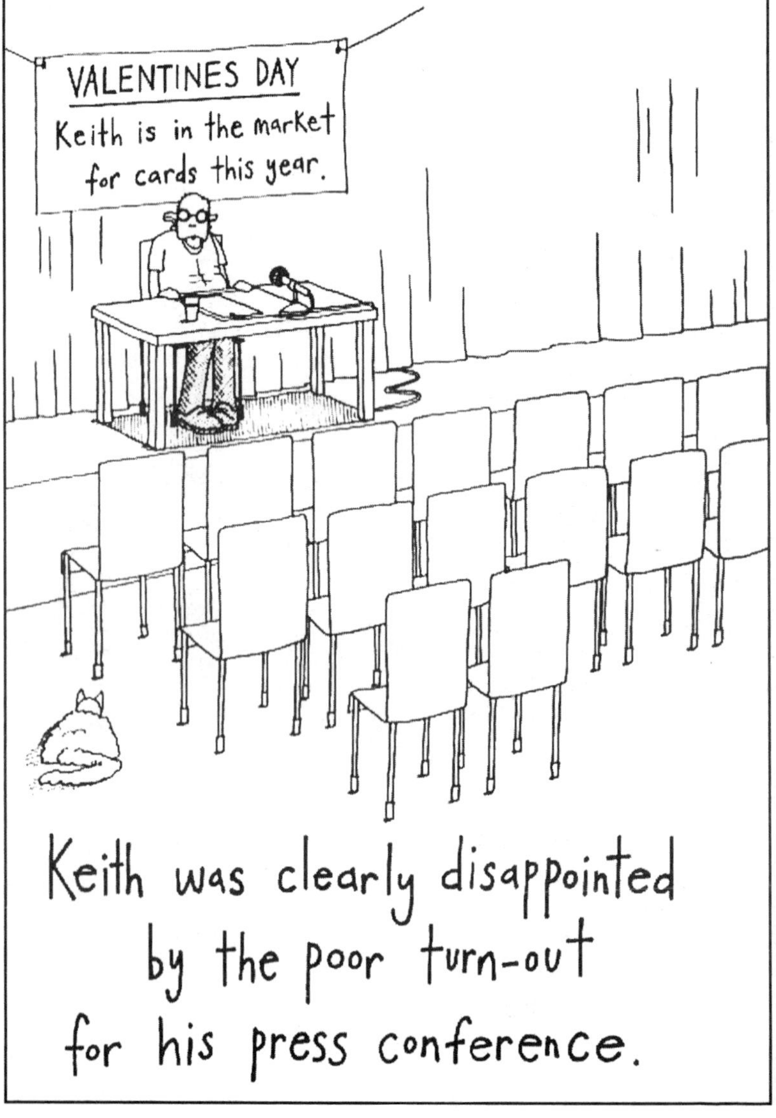
VALENTINES DAY
Keith is in the market for cards this year.

Keith was clearly disappointed by the poor turn-out for his press conference.

It was early Spring, and time
to start bromiding Vern's
tea again.

Tips for Crush-free
Yuletide Commuting

No. 38 The wild eyes, dribbly grin and mistletoe routine.

What baggage handlers
do for kicks.

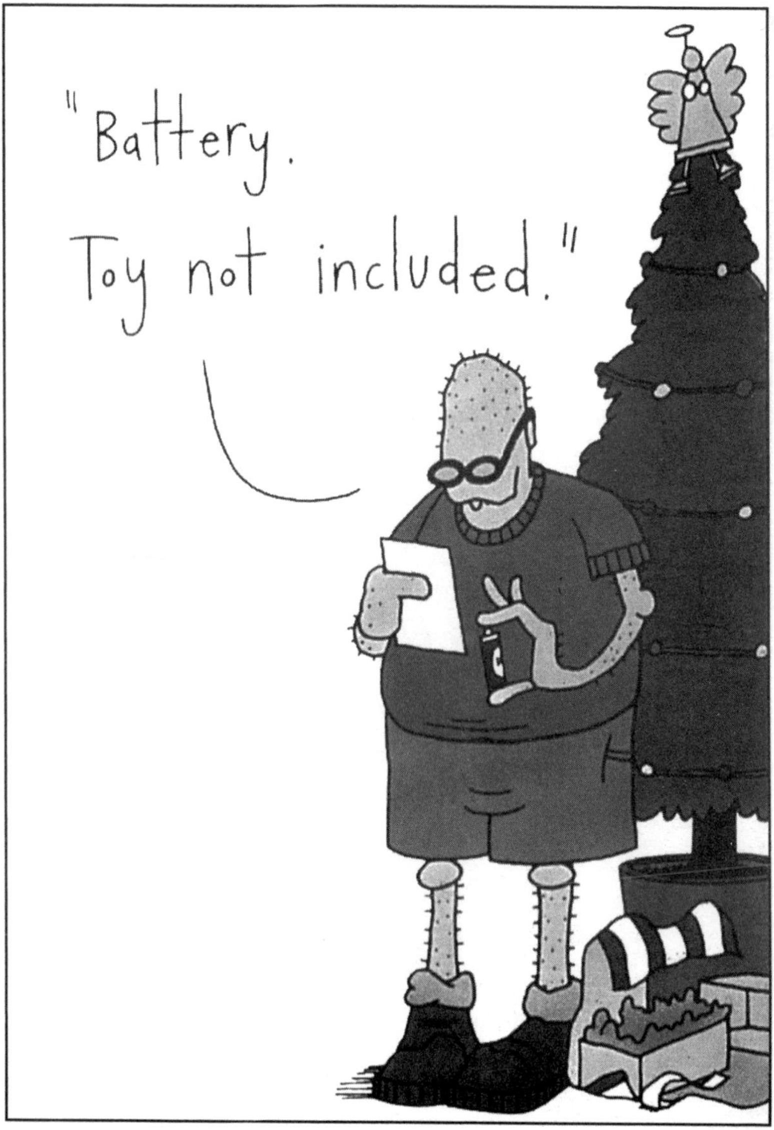
"Battery.
Toy not included."

"**Right!** That's it, Billy — you're grounded. I specifically told you **not** to ignite your grandmother's farts."

In a tragic failure to grasp the Firework Code, Ralph puts all of his pets into a box with a tight-fitting lid.

"Hmm, a **penis fixation** you say?
Why don't you hang up your
coat and hat, and
I'll be right with you."

Tracy had managed to smuggle
her father in as a
lucky gonk.

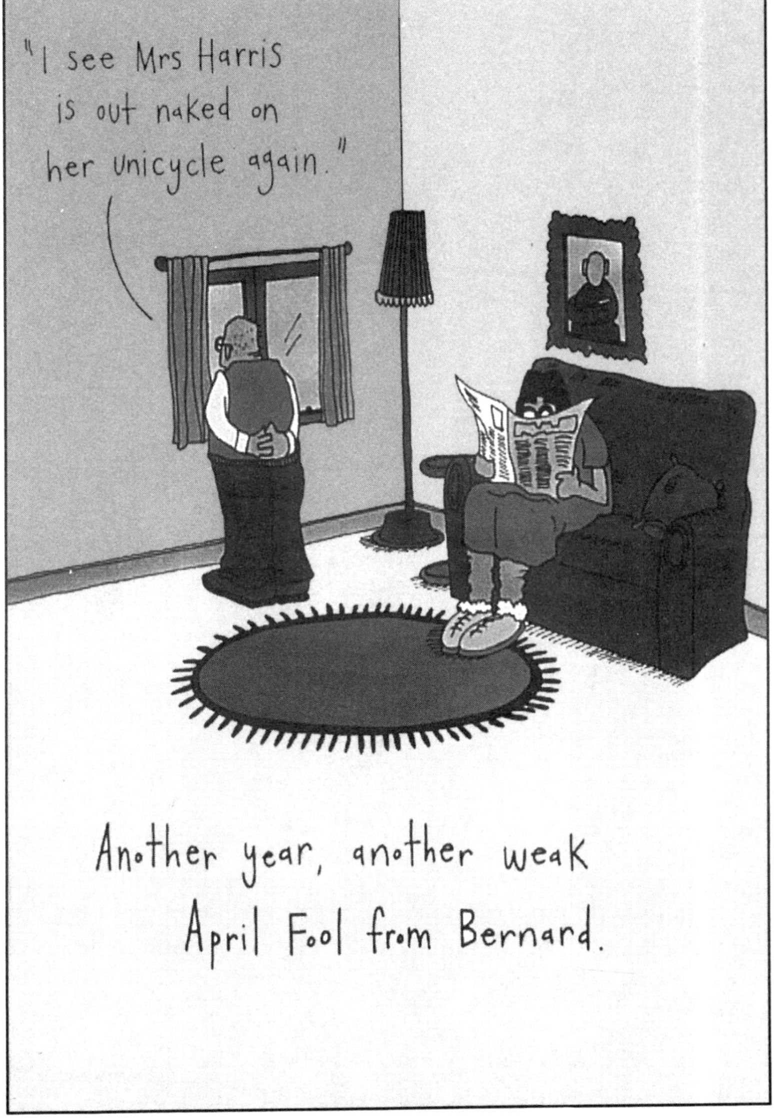
"I see Mrs Harris is out naked on her unicycle again."
Another year, another weak April Fool from Bernard.

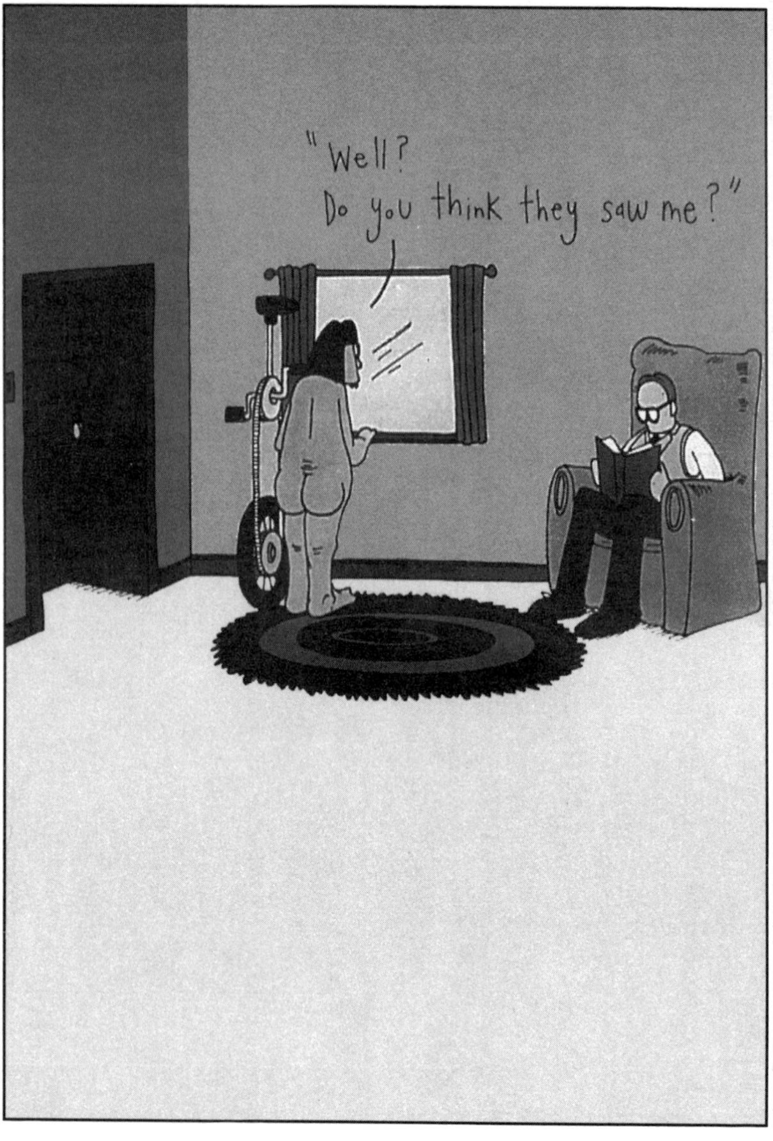
"Well?
Do you think they saw me?"

The Lumbermeister 350
had improved Darren's
Treat/Trick ratio no end.

"check the map, guys —
we've got twin girls here."

Derek's Valentines Night
check-list always
made Norma nervous.

The majority of the cartoons in this book are available as a stunning collection of full colour Greeting cards from all good Greeting card retailers

PUBLISHED BY

NIGEL QUINEY PUBLICATIONS